Contents

1 Introduction

Line is the fundamental building block of visual art. It defines shapes, creates textures, implies movement, and evokes emotion. In its simplest form, a line is a mark made by a tool across a surface. Yet, within this simplicity lies immense expressive potential. This book explores the dynamic interplay of line in pen and brush drawing, offering a journey into the world of fluid linework, rhythmic hatching, and expressive mark-making. We will discover how to wield these tools to create drawings that are not only technically proficient but also vibrantly alive with energy and emotion. From the delicate whisper of a fine pen line to the bold sweep of a loaded brush, each mark carries the potential for dynamic expression. This exploration invites you to embrace the versatility of line and unlock its artistic power.

Central to this journey are the tools of the trade. Selecting the right materials is essential for achieving the desired effects in your artwork. For pens, consider exploring a range of nib sizes and types. Fine-tipped pens, such as technical pens or Micron pens, offer precision and control for intricate details and delicate lines. Broader nibs, found in calligraphy pens or markers, allow for bolder strokes and expressive variations in line weight. Experimenting with different pen types will help you discover the nuances of each and expand your artistic vocabulary. Similarly, brush selection plays a critical role in shaping your brushwork. Round brushes are versatile for both detailed work and broader strokes, while flat brushes excel at creating sharp edges and consistent washes. Consider exploring different bristle types, such as sable, synthetic, or hog bristle, each offering unique characteristics in terms of stiffness, absorbency, and resilience. The choice of ink also impacts the final result. Traditional India ink is known for its rich black and permanence, while drawing inks come in a wider range of colors and offer varying degrees of water resistance. Experimentation is key to finding the combinations that best suit your style and artistic vision.

Creating a dedicated workspace is paramount for fostering creativity and concentration. A well-organized and comfortable setup allows you to focus on the process of drawing without distractions. Ideally, your workspace should have ample natural light, a comfortable chair that supports good posture, and a drawing surface at a suitable height. Keep your pens, brushes, inks, and other materials organized and readily accessible. A simple storage system, such as a desk organizer or drawer dividers, can help maintain order and prevent clutter from hindering your creative flow. Consider personalizing your workspace with elements that inspire you, such as artwork, plants, or objects that hold personal significance. A clutter-free and inspiring environment will set the stage for focused and productive drawing sessions. This initial preparation will empower you to embark on your creative journey with confidence and enthusiasm.

Paper selection is another crucial aspect of your artistic toolkit. The texture, weight, and absorbency of the paper significantly influence how your pen and brush strokes appear. Smooth paper surfaces are ideal for detailed work and fine lines, allowing for precise control and minimal feathering. Textured papers, such as watercolor paper or drawing paper with a tooth, offer a different kind of interaction with your tools. The texture can create interesting variations in line quality and add depth to your drawings. Experiment with different paper weights as well, keeping in mind that heavier papers can handle more layering and washes without buckling. As you gain experience, you'll develop a preference for certain paper types based on your individual style and the desired effects. Exploring different papers expands your artistic possibilities and allows you to tailor your materials to your specific creative goals.

Ultimately, the most valuable tools are patience and practice. Developing proficiency in pen and brush techniques takes time and dedication. Embrace the learning process, and don't be afraid to experiment and make mistakes. Each stroke, whether successful or not, contributes to your growth as an artist. Observe the lines you create, analyze their qualities, and reflect on how you can refine your technique. Through consistent practice and a willingness to explore, you will gradually gain mastery over your tools and develop a unique artistic voice. This journey of exploration and experimentation is at the heart of expressive linework. It's about discovering the dynamic potential of pen and brush, uncovering the nuances of each mark, and ultimately, finding your own artistic language.

1.1 The Essence of Line

A line is more than just a mark connecting two points. It's a fundamental element of visual language, capable of conveying a wealth of information and emotion. Think about it: a single, unwavering line can represent stability, a jagged line suggests chaos, and a delicate, curving line whispers of elegance. In this chapter, we'll unravel the essence of line, exploring its potential as a powerful tool for artistic expression. We'll discover how lines, in their various forms, can breathe life into your drawings, giving them depth, character, and dynamic energy. This understanding will form the bedrock for all subsequent chapters, shaping your approach to pen and brush work.

Consider the sheer variety of lines you encounter every day: the sharp edges of buildings against the sky, the delicate veins of a leaf, the tangled wires criss-crossing overhead. Each line possesses its own unique quality, determined by its weight, direction, and texture. Observe these lines closely, noticing how they interact with each other and with the surrounding space. This careful observation is the first step towards mastering linework in your own art. Begin to see the world as a network of interconnected lines, each telling its own silent story.

Now, translate this observation to your drawing practice. Instead of simply outlining shapes, think about how you can use lines to describe the essence of your subject. Imagine drawing a drape of fabric. Rather than using a single, uniform line to define its edge, try using a series of varying lines to capture its folds and creases. A heavier line can indicate a deep shadow, while a lighter, more hesitant line can suggest a gentle curve. By varying the pressure and speed of your hand, you can create lines that are full of life and character.

Experiment with different types of lines: long, short, thick, thin, straight, curved, jagged, smooth. Each type of line evokes a different feeling and can be used to create a specific effect. A series of short, staccato lines can create a sense of texture or tension, while a long, flowing line can suggest grace and movement. Don't be afraid to push the boundaries of what a line can be. Let your lines dance across the page, expressing the rhythm and energy of your subject.

Think of the masters of linework, artists like Rembrandt or Leonardo da Vinci. Their drawings are not just accurate representations of their subjects; they are expressions of their understanding of form, light, and shadow. Study their work, paying attention to how they use line to create volume and depth. Notice how they use hatching and cross-hatching to build up layers of tone and texture. Emulate their techniques, but don't simply copy them. Instead, use them as inspiration to develop your own unique style.

The essence of line extends beyond its descriptive qualities. Lines can also be used to create abstract compositions, exploring the interplay of positive and negative space. Think about the work of artists like Paul Klee or Wassily Kandinsky, who used line to create dynamic and evocative abstract works. They demonstrated that lines, when arranged in certain ways, can evoke emotions and ideas without necessarily representing recognizable objects.

Remember that the mastery of line is a journey, not a destination. It requires patience, practice, and a willingness to experiment. Don't be discouraged if your early attempts don't meet your expectations. Every line you draw, whether successful or not, is a learning experience. Embrace the process of exploration and allow yourself to make mistakes. It is through these mistakes that you will discover new possibilities and refine your skills.

As you progress, you will develop a deeper understanding of the nuances of line. You'll learn to control the pressure and speed of your hand to create lines of varying weight and texture. You'll discover how to use lines to create the illusion of form and volume. And most importantly, you'll begin to develop your own unique style, a visual language that is uniquely yours.

The beauty of line lies in its simplicity and versatility. With a single pen or brush, you can create a world of visual possibilities. So, pick up your tools, embrace the power of the line, and begin your journey of artistic exploration. Let your hand move freely across the page, allowing the lines to flow from your imagination onto the paper. This is where the true magic of drawing begins. The journey of understanding and mastering line is a lifelong pursuit, a constant dialogue between your hand, your eye, and your imagination.

1.2 Tools and Materials

Selecting the right tools and materials is paramount to achieving fluidity and expressiveness in your linework. This chapter will equip you with the knowledge to make informed choices about the pens, brushes, inks, and paper that will best suit your artistic journey. Think of these tools as extensions of your own creativity, each with unique characteristics and potential waiting to be unlocked.

Let's start with pens. For fluid linework, a responsive pen that allows for subtle pressure variations is essential. Consider exploring fountain pens with different nib sizes and flex. A fine nib is excellent for intricate details and delicate lines, while a broader nib allows for bold, expressive strokes and dramatic variations in line weight. Dip pens, with their interchangeable nibs, offer an even wider range of possibilities, from crisp, sharp lines to broad, calligraphic strokes. Experiment with different nibs to discover the effects you enjoy most. Don't overlook the readily available technical drawing pens. These pens, with their consistent ink flow and precise line widths, are ideal for controlled hatching and detailed work, providing a different kind of control than the more fluid fountain or dip pens.

Moving on to brushes, the options are equally diverse. Round brushes, with their pointed tips, are versatile tools for both fine lines and broader washes, depending on the pressure applied and the angle at which the brush is held. Flat brushes, on the other hand, create bold, even strokes and are particularly well-suited for washes and creating textural effects. Experiment with synthetic and natural hair brushes to find what feels most comfortable in your hand and yields the desired effects. Consider the size and shape of the brush in relation to the scale of your drawings. Smaller brushes are ideal for detail work, while larger brushes excel at covering larger areas and creating expressive washes.

Ink plays a crucial role in the final appearance of your linework. Traditional India ink offers a rich, deep black, known for its permanence and resistance to fading. However, a world of other inks awaits, each with unique properties. Explore different colors and consider how they can enhance your drawings, evoking different moods and adding another layer of expression. Test the ink's flow characteristics on scrap paper to understand how it behaves with your chosen pen or brush. Some inks are more fluid, while others are thicker and more resistant, offering different possibilities for texture and line quality. Waterproof inks are essential if you plan to layer washes over your pen work, preventing the lines from bleeding or blurring.

The paper you choose is the foundation of your artwork, and its texture and weight significantly impact the final result. Smooth paper allows for crisp, clean lines and detailed work. Rougher paper, however, can add a unique texture to your lines, creating interesting variations and a more organic feel. Experiment with different paper weights as well. Heavier paper can handle multiple layers of ink and washes without buckling, while lighter paper is more suited for quick sketches and studies. Consider the size and format of your paper in relation to the subject matter and the overall composition you envision.

Beyond these core tools, several other materials can enhance your drawing experience. A good quality eraser is essential for correcting mistakes and lifting out highlights. A kneaded eraser is particularly useful for gently lightening areas without completely removing the lines. A ruler or straight edge can be helpful for creating precise lines and geometric shapes, especially when working on architectural drawings or designs. A drawing board provides a stable surface to work on, preventing the paper from slipping and ensuring even pressure across your lines. Finally, a lightbox can be invaluable for transferring sketches or tracing images, allowing you to refine your compositions before committing them to ink.

Don't be afraid to experiment and find what combination of tools and materials best suits your personal style. The joy of drawing lies not only in the final product but also in the process of discovery and experimentation. Embrace the possibilities, allow yourself to make mistakes, and celebrate the unique qualities that each tool and material brings to your artistic expression. By carefully considering these elements, you are setting the stage for a fulfilling and expressive journey into the world of fluid linework. Remember, the materials are just the starting point, your artistic vision and skillful application are what truly bring the lines to life.

1.3 Setting Up Your Workspace

Your creative space doesn't need to be a grand artist's studio bathed in northern light. A small corner of a quiet room, a kitchen table cleared for action, or even a portable setup for drawing on the go—all are perfectly valid. The key is to create an environment that fosters focus and allows you to comfortably engage with your materials. Think practically. Where will you store your pens, brushes, and inks? A simple desk organizer, a repurposed toolbox, or even a few well-chosen jars can keep your tools within easy reach and prevent accidental spills. Consider your lighting. Natural light is ideal, offering true color representation and reducing eye strain. If natural light is limited, invest in a good quality desk lamp that mimics natural daylight. Position your light source to avoid casting shadows across your drawing surface. Experiment with different placements to find what works best for you. Left-handed artists may prefer the light source on the right to prevent their hand from casting a shadow, while right-handed artists might prefer the opposite. Don't be afraid to adjust your lighting as needed throughout your drawing session.

A comfortable chair is essential for longer drawing periods. Choose a chair that supports your back and allows you to maintain good posture. A slight recline can be beneficial for preventing backaches and promoting a relaxed drawing position. If your workspace involves a table, ensure it's at a comfortable height. You shouldn't have to hunch over your work, as this can lead to discomfort and restrict the fluidity of your linework. Experiment with different table heights or consider using a drawing board that can be angled to suit your preference.

Now, let's talk about surfaces. While a simple pad of drawing paper is sufficient for practice and experimentation, exploring different paper types can greatly enhance your linework. Smooth paper allows for crisp, clean lines and is particularly well-suited for detailed pen work. Textured paper, on the other hand, can add a unique dimension to your drawings, catching the ink in interesting ways and creating varied line qualities. Experiment with different paper weights, textures, and finishes to discover what best suits your style and the type of linework you aim to create. Keep a variety of papers on hand to explore different effects.

Organization extends beyond just your immediate workspace. How will you store your finished drawings? A portfolio or dedicated folder will protect your work and keep it organized. Consider a filing system that allows you to categorize your drawings by subject, technique, or date. This will not only protect your work but also make it easier to review your progress and identify areas for growth. Documenting your journey is a valuable part of the creative process.

Beyond the physical setup, consider the ambiance of your workspace. What inspires you? Perhaps it's a piece of music, a particular scent, or a view from your window. Incorporate elements that foster creativity and a sense of calm. A clutter-free workspace can promote a clear mind, while a few carefully chosen objects or images can spark inspiration. For some, a quiet environment is crucial for concentration, while others thrive with background music or ambient noise. Experiment to discover what helps you enter a state of flow.

Remember, your workspace is an extension of your creative self. It should be a place where you feel comfortable, inspired, and free to experiment. Don't be afraid to personalize your space with elements that resonate with you. A small plant, a favorite mug, or a collection of inspiring artwork can make your workspace feel more inviting and conducive to creative exploration. Regularly assess your workspace and make adjustments as needed. Your needs and preferences may change over time, so it's important to adapt your environment to support your evolving artistic practice.

Ultimately, the most important aspect of setting up your workspace is creating an environment that supports your creative process. There's no one-size-fits-all solution. What works for one artist may not work for another. The key is to experiment, adapt, and personalize your space to create a sanctuary for your artistic endeavors. Pay attention to the details that enhance your focus and inspire your creativity. By creating a dedicated and personalized workspace, you'll be well-equipped to embark on your journey of exploring fluid linework in pen and brush.

2 Basic Line Control

Control over your line is the cornerstone of expressive drawing. Think of the line not merely as a descriptive tool, but as a living entity with its own energy and personality. This chapter explores two fundamental aspects of line control: pressure and weight, and speed and rhythm. Mastering these elements will unlock a world of possibilities in your linework, allowing you to create drawings that pulsate with life and dynamism.

Pressure, applied with varying degrees of force, directly impacts the weight of your line—its visual thickness and density. A light touch produces delicate, almost ethereal lines, whispering across the page. Increasing pressure yields bolder, more assertive marks, commanding attention. This interplay between subtle whispers and powerful declarations is a powerful tool. Imagine drawing a leaf: a delicate, light pressure line traces the edges, while heavier pressure defines the veins and stem, giving the impression of structure and life. Practice varying your pressure consciously, observing the resulting changes in line quality. Experiment with gradual transitions from light to heavy and vice versa within a single stroke. This control allows you to create depth, emphasis, and a sense of three-dimensionality even in simple line drawings.

Speed and rhythm are equally vital in imbuing your lines with character. A slow, deliberate stroke creates a steady, controlled line, conveying a sense of calmness and precision. Rapid strokes, on the other hand, result in looser, more energetic lines, suggesting movement and spontaneity. Just as a musician varies tempo and rhythm to create a melody, you can modulate the speed of your strokes to introduce dynamism and variety into your drawings. Try drawing a series of parallel lines, alternating between slow, deliberate strokes and quick, gestural ones. Notice how the varying speeds create a visual rhythm, adding interest and energy to the otherwise simple pattern.

Now, let's delve deeper into the practical application of these principles. Consider a simple subject like a flowing drape. To capture its graceful folds and curves, vary your pressure and speed in accordance with the form. Use lighter, faster strokes to depict the areas where the fabric flows freely, and heavier, slower strokes to emphasize the areas where it bunches or folds. This interplay of line weight and speed will create a sense of volume and movement, bringing the drape to life on the page.

Further exploration of pressure can lead to the creation of lines that taper elegantly at both ends. This technique, often used in calligraphy and expressive drawing, adds a refined touch to your linework. It requires a subtle shift in pressure as you begin and end each stroke, gradually increasing pressure as the line emerges and then gradually decreasing it as the line fades away. Practice this technique with simple curves and spirals, focusing on achieving smooth, controlled transitions in line weight. Imagine drawing a bird's feather: the tapering lines can perfectly capture its delicate, almost weightless quality.

Rhythm in linework can also be explored through the use of broken lines, where a continuous line is replaced by a series of shorter, interconnected strokes. This technique can be used to suggest texture, movement, or even emotion. A series of short, choppy strokes might convey the rough texture of bark, while longer, more flowing broken lines might suggest the gentle sway of grass in the wind. Experiment with different lengths and spacing of broken lines to see how they impact the overall feel of your drawing.

Finally, consider how pressure and speed work together to create truly dynamic lines. Imagine drawing a gust of wind. You might start with light, fast strokes to represent the initial rush of air, then gradually increase pressure and slow down your strokes as the wind builds in intensity. By combining variations in both pressure and speed, you can create lines that not only depict the form of the wind, but also convey its force and energy. This symbiotic relationship between pressure and speed is key to unlocking the full expressive potential of your lines. Practice these techniques regularly, and you'll discover a wealth of possibilities in the seemingly simple act of drawing a line. Don't be afraid to experiment, to push the boundaries of what a line can be. With dedicated practice, you'll develop a mastery of line control that will elevate your drawings to new levels of dynamism and expression.

2.1 Pressure and Weight

The feeling of the pen or brush in your hand, the subtle shift in pressure as you draw across the page—these seemingly small actions are the foundation of expressive linework. Pressure, in the context of drawing, isn't simply about how hard you press, but also about the nuanced control you exert over your tool. It's the deliberate modulation of force that breathes life into your lines, transforming them from static marks into dynamic strokes that communicate weight, depth, and emotion. Think of a tightrope walker carefully adjusting their balance – the subtle shifts in weight maintain equilibrium. Similarly, adjusting the pressure on your pen or brush allows you to control the thickness, value, and character of your lines, creating a visual balance and rhythm in your work.

Begin by experimenting with a simple exercise: gradually increasing pressure as you draw a horizontal line, then gradually decreasing it. Repeat this with vertical, diagonal, and curved lines. Notice how the line swells and tapers, responding directly to the pressure you apply. This basic principle—controlling line weight through pressure—is a cornerstone of fluid linework. This exercise might seem rudimentary, but mastering this fundamental control unlocks a world of expressive possibilities. Imagine drawing a blade of grass – a delicate, tapering line captures its fragility, while a thicker, more forceful stroke suggests the sturdy stem of a sunflower.

Consider the weight of an object as a visual representation of its mass. A heavier object appears to exert more force on its surroundings. We can translate this concept to our drawings by using varying line weights to convey the perceived weight of different elements. A heavier line naturally suggests more weight, while a lighter line implies delicacy. Observe the world around you: the thick, sturdy trunk of an oak tree compared to the delicate petals of a flower. Translate these observations into your linework, using thicker lines to depict the weighty trunk and thinner lines for the fragile petals.

This principle also applies to the depiction of shadows. The darker areas of a shadow often suggest greater weight or depth. By applying more pressure to your pen or brush in these darker regions, you can create richer, more saturated lines that visually reinforce the depth and solidity of the cast shadow. Conversely, as the shadow transitions to lighter areas, lessen the pressure to create thinner, more delicate lines, thus capturing the subtle gradations of tone and form.

Think about the direction of your strokes as they relate to the form you are drawing. When drawing a curved surface, for instance, try varying your pressure along the curve. As the curve turns away from the light source, apply slightly more pressure to create a darker, heavier line, suggesting the transition into shadow. As the curve turns toward the light, lighten your pressure to create a thinner, lighter line, highlighting the area where light strikes the surface. This subtle variation in line weight can dramatically enhance the three-dimensionality of your drawing.

Experiment with different types of pens and brushes to further explore the relationship between pressure and line weight. A flexible nib pen will respond dramatically to changes in pressure, producing a wide range of line variations. A stiff nib, on the other hand, offers more control and precision for finer lines. Similarly, different brushes will react uniquely to pressure, depending on their bristle type and stiffness. Experimentation is key to understanding how each tool responds to your touch.

Practicing with different tools and observing how they interact with the paper expands your understanding of pressure and control. You'll discover that each combination of tool and paper offers a unique set of expressive possibilities. A rough-textured paper, for example, will create a broken, textured line when used with a dry pen, while a smooth paper allows for a clean, continuous stroke. This interplay between tool, paper, and pressure provides a rich vocabulary for expressing your artistic vision.

Don't limit yourself to thinking of pressure simply in terms of thick and thin lines. Explore the expressive potential of broken lines, textured lines, and varying degrees of opacity. A lightly applied, broken line can suggest a delicate texture or a sense of fleeting movement. A heavily applied, textured line can convey roughness, age, or strength.

As you continue to experiment, you will develop a deeper understanding of the subtle nuances of pressure and how it can be used to create truly dynamic and expressive linework. Remember, the goal is not to rigidly adhere to rules, but to develop a sensitivity to the relationship between your hand, the tool, and the surface. Through consistent practice and mindful observation, you will cultivate a refined control of pressure, transforming your lines into powerful tools for artistic expression. This control, this intimate understanding of pressure and weight, will ultimately empower you to create drawings that resonate with depth, character, and life.

2.2 Speed and Rhythm

Controlling the speed of your pen or brush is akin to a dancer controlling their pace across the floor: sometimes a swift dash, other times a slow, deliberate step. This control is fundamental to creating dynamic and expressive linework. A rapid stroke imbues a line with energy and lightness, suggesting movement and spontaneity. A slower, more measured stroke conveys weight and deliberation, hinting at solidity and form. Mastering this interplay between speed and rhythm is crucial for breathing life into your drawings. Practice varying your speed consciously, observing how it affects the character of your lines. Experiment with quick, gestural strokes to capture the essence of a fleeting moment, then contrast them with slow, deliberate lines that define the contours of an object. This conscious variation injects dynamism and visual interest into your work.

Think of a bird in flight. Its wings beat rapidly, a blur of motion, as it ascends swiftly. Then, as it circles, preparing to land, the wing beats slow, each movement precise and controlled. Your lines can mimic this same variation in speed and energy. A fast, sweeping line across the page can depict the rush of wind through leaves, while a series of slow, deliberate hatches can build the solid form of a tree trunk. This conscious control of speed allows you to communicate not just what you see, but also the feeling and energy of your subject. By modulating your pace, you can create lines that are both descriptive and expressive, capturing the essence of your subject matter.

Rhythm, too, plays a vital role in dynamic linework. It's the underlying beat, the pattern of movement that gives your drawing a sense of flow and cohesion. Just as a musician uses rhythm to create a melody, an artist uses it to create visual harmony. Rhythm can be established through the repetition of lines, the variation of their lengths and thicknesses, and the spacing between them. A regular, consistent rhythm can create a sense of calm and order, while a more irregular, syncopated rhythm can evoke excitement and movement. Explore different rhythmic patterns in your drawings. Try repeating a series of short, quick strokes followed by a long, flowing line. Observe how the varying rhythm impacts the overall feel of your piece. This exploration will help you develop a sensitivity to the rhythmic possibilities of line, allowing you to create drawings that are visually engaging and dynamically balanced.

Consider a winding road cutting through a landscape. The lines depicting the road might be long and flowing in some sections, short and staccato in others, reflecting the curves and bends of its path. This variation in line length and direction creates a visual rhythm that guides the viewer's eye through the drawing. Similarly, when hatching, vary the length and spacing of your lines to create different textural effects. Closely spaced, uniform lines create a smooth, dense texture, while loosely spaced, varied lines suggest a rougher, more textured surface. By mastering the interplay of length, spacing, and direction, you imbue your drawings with a sense of rhythm and depth, transforming flat lines into a rich tapestry of textures and forms.

Experiment with different combinations of speed and rhythm. Try drawing a series of parallel lines, gradually increasing your speed with each line. Then, reverse the process, slowing down with each subsequent line. Observe how the changing speed affects the weight and energy of the lines. This simple exercise helps you develop a kinesthetic awareness of how your hand movements translate into visual marks on the page. Next, try varying the spacing between the lines, creating rhythmic patterns that enhance the visual interest of your drawing. Perhaps you create a dense cluster of lines in one area, then a wide, open space in another. This deliberate manipulation of speed, rhythm, and spacing transforms simple lines into a powerful tool for artistic expression.

Practicing with different tools further refines your control over speed and rhythm. A fine-tipped pen lends itself to precise, controlled lines, ideal for detailed work and intricate hatching. A broader nib allows for greater variation in line weight and encourages more fluid, expressive strokes. Similarly, different brushes offer unique possibilities. A stiff-bristled brush creates a textured, broken line, while a soft brush allows for smooth, flowing washes. Explore the capabilities of each tool, paying attention to how it responds to changes in speed and pressure. This exploration will expand your repertoire of mark-making techniques and enrich your artistic vocabulary.

Imagine drawing a delicate flower petal with a fine-tipped pen. The slow, controlled movements allow you to capture the subtle curves and delicate veins of the petal. Now, switch to a broad brush loaded with ink, and depict the energetic splash of a wave crashing against a rock. The rapid, sweeping movements of the brush capture the force and fluidity of the water. By understanding the unique properties of each tool, you can choose the one that best suits your subject matter and desired effect. This mindful selection of tools, combined with a mastery of speed and rhythm, allows you to create drawings that are not only visually compelling but also deeply expressive.

3 Advanced Linework

Mastering advanced linework elevates your drawings from simple sketches to dynamic and expressive pieces. This chapter focuses on refining your control over line, exploring its potential to create texture, depth, and movement. We'll delve into techniques like cross-hatching, layering, and using line to suggest form and perspective, giving your artwork a three-dimensional quality and a sense of dynamism. Prepare to transform your lines from mere outlines into powerful tools of artistic expression.

Texture is essential for conveying the tactile qualities of a subject. Imagine drawing a rough stone wall. Simply outlining the stones won't capture their ruggedness. By employing varying line weights, short, broken lines, and dense clusters of marks, you can create the illusion of a textured surface. Consider the direction of the lines as well. Lines that follow the contours of the object enhance the sense of three-dimensionality and texture, bringing your drawing to life. Practice creating different textures – smooth, rough, bumpy, furry – using various line techniques. Experiment with different pen nibs and pressures to discover a wider range of textural effects.

Cross-hatching and layering are powerful techniques for building depth and volume. Cross-hatching involves layering sets of parallel lines over each other at varying angles. The density of the lines creates the illusion of shadow and form. Where lines are closer together, the area appears darker, receding into the background. Conversely, areas with fewer lines appear lighter, giving the impression of highlights and projecting forms forward. Layering, a similar technique, utilizes overlapping lines to achieve depth, but without the strict parallel structure of cross-hatching. This can create a more organic and less structured effect. Try combining cross-hatching and layering to create complex and nuanced shading, experimenting with different line weights and directions to achieve a range of tonal values.

Implying form and volume relies on understanding how light interacts with objects. Observe how light creates highlights and shadows on a simple object, like a sphere. Use lighter, thinner lines to depict the highlighted areas and denser, darker lines for the shadowed areas. The gradual transition from light to dark creates the illusion of a curved surface. Practice drawing basic geometric shapes like cubes, cones, and cylinders, focusing on using line to convey their three-dimensionality. Remember to consider the light source and how it affects the shading and form of the object.

Perspective is crucial for creating realistic and believable scenes. One-point perspective, where lines converge towards a single vanishing point, is a fundamental principle. Practice drawing simple structures like buildings or roads, using converging lines to create the illusion of depth. Two-point perspective, with two vanishing points, offers a more dynamic representation of objects. Experiment with both one-point and two-point perspective to understand how they affect the spatial relationships within your drawings. Use lighter lines further away and darker lines closer, to create depth with perspective lines.

Dynamic movement can be captured through the use of directional lines and gestural strokes. Imagine drawing a dancer mid-leap. Instead of static outlines, use flowing, curved lines that follow the movement of the body. Vary the line weight to emphasize the force and energy of the motion. Thicker lines suggest strength and power, while thinner lines convey grace and lightness. Practice drawing subjects in motion – animals running, birds flying, or people gesturing – using dynamic lines to capture their energy and fluidity. Don't be afraid to exaggerate the lines and curves to amplify the sense of movement.

Experiment with different types of line. A continuous, unbroken line can create a sense of elegance and flow. Short, choppy lines convey a different feeling, perhaps one of tension or excitement. Zigzagging lines can express energy or chaos. Explore the expressive possibilities of different line types and how they can contribute to the overall mood and message of your drawings. By combining all these techniques, you can create rich, layered drawings that are full of life and movement. Remember that practice is key to mastering these skills. The more you experiment with line, the more confident and expressive your drawings will become.

Through conscious application of these principles, your linework will transcend its descriptive function and become a powerful tool for expressing depth, texture, and movement. Remember, the key is not just to depict what you see, but to capture the essence of your subject and convey your unique artistic vision. Don't be afraid to push the boundaries of line, to experiment, and to discover new ways of expressing yourself through this fundamental element of art. Practice capturing the essence of your subject matter with simple, yet descriptive lines and don't be hesitant to vary their thickness to communicate volume and form effectively.

3.1 Creating Textures

Texture, in the context of linework, isn't about the tactile feel of a surface. Instead, it's the illusion of texture, the visual impression of roughness, smoothness, or pattern created entirely through the manipulation of lines. We achieve this by varying line weight, direction, and density. Think of a drawing of a tree trunk. You wouldn't simply draw an outline. You'd use lines to suggest the rough bark, perhaps short, jagged lines clustered together in areas, longer, flowing lines elsewhere, creating a visual sense of texture. This chapter will delve into the methods of achieving these effects using both pen and brush.

One of the most fundamental ways to create texture with line is through hatching and cross-hatching. Hatching uses parallel lines to suggest shading and form. The closer the lines, the darker the area appears, creating a sense of density and shadow. Cross-hatching takes this a step further by layering sets of parallel lines at different angles, increasing the darkness and complexity of the texture. Experiment with the spacing and direction of your hatching lines. Vary the pressure on your pen or brush to create thicker or thinner lines within the hatched area, adding another layer of visual interest and realism. Imagine depicting the woven texture of a basket using carefully placed cross-hatching, the intersecting lines mimicking the interwoven strands.

Stippling offers another avenue for creating textural effects. This technique involves using dots to build up tone and texture. A dense cluster of dots creates a dark area, while sparsely placed dots suggest a lighter tone. Stippling can be incredibly effective for creating textures like pebbled surfaces, or the grainy texture of sand. Consider varying the size and shape of the dots themselves. A combination of small, tight dots and larger, more loosely placed dots can add a dynamic and organic feel to the texture. Practice stippling with different pen nibs to see how they impact the resulting texture. A fine-nibbed pen will create delicate, precise dots, while a broader nib will produce bolder, more graphic marks.

Moving beyond individual techniques, consider how combinations of linework can create even more complex textures. Imagine depicting the fur of an animal. You might use a combination of long, flowing lines to suggest the overall direction of the fur, layered with shorter, finer lines to create the illusion of individual hairs. Incorporate stippling to add depth and shadow within the fur, further enhancing the textural effect. Don't be afraid to experiment with different combinations of techniques to discover new and interesting textural possibilities. The key is to observe the textures around you and try to replicate them using lines.

Brushwork introduces another dimension to texture creation. The flexibility of a brush allows for a wider range of line qualities, from thin, delicate strokes to broad, expressive washes. Dry brush techniques, where the brush is loaded with minimal ink or paint, can create scratchy, textured effects, perfect for depicting weathered surfaces or dry foliage. Experiment with different brush angles and pressures to discover the variety of marks you can make. Think about how you can use brushstrokes to create the illusion of different materials, like the smooth, reflective surface of water or the rough, porous texture of stone.

Combining pen and brush allows for an even greater range of textural expression. Use pen to create fine details and precise lines, then layer washes of ink or paint with a brush to add depth and atmosphere. The contrast between the crisp, defined pen lines and the softer, more diffuse brushstrokes can create a rich and dynamic texture. Imagine drawing a cityscape with detailed pen lines for the buildings and then using washes of ink to create the atmospheric perspective and the texture of the sky.

Remember, creating texture with line is all about observation and experimentation. Look closely at the world around you. Study the textures of different materials, the way light plays across surfaces, the intricate patterns found in nature. Then, try to replicate those textures using the techniques we've discussed. Don't be afraid to experiment with different line weights, directions, densities, and combinations of pen and brush. The more you practice, the more adept you will become at creating convincing and compelling textures in your drawings. Your sketchbook should be a playground for exploration. Fill it with experiments, trying different combinations of techniques, and pushing the boundaries of what you can achieve with line.

3.2 Cross-Hatching & Layering

Cross-hatching, at its simplest, is the layering of lines over one another at various angles to create value, texture, and form. Think of it as building a structure with lines, each stroke adding to the overall strength and complexity of the image. Start with a light touch, laying down your initial lines in one direction. These foundational lines should follow the contours of the subject, defining its underlying structure. Imagine drawing a simple sphere: your initial lines might curve gently around its form, subtly suggesting its roundness. Don't press too hard; these first strokes are merely the scaffolding.

Once you've established this initial layer, begin adding a second layer of lines at a different angle. A common approach is to cross the initial lines at a roughly 45-degree angle, but feel free to experiment. The intersection of these lines begins to build up density, creating areas of darker value. Notice how the overlapping lines create small diamond shapes. The smaller and more densely packed these diamonds, the darker the value will appear. This interplay of light and dark is key to achieving a sense of three-dimensionality. Consider the sphere again: by cross-hatching along its curves, you begin to define the areas where light falls and where shadows deepen, giving the illusion of volume.

Layering expands upon this concept, moving beyond simple cross-hatching to incorporate multiple layers of lines at varying angles, pressures, and even with different tools. Instead of just two intersecting layers, imagine building up a network of lines, each contributing to the overall texture and depth. This allows for incredibly subtle gradations of tone and texture. Think of the way a weaver creates complex patterns by interlacing different threads. Similarly, you can layer lines to build a rich tapestry of values, creating the illusion of smooth transitions from light to dark.

With layering, you're not limited to straight lines. Introduce curved lines, hatched lines, and even broken lines to add further complexity and visual interest. Imagine drawing a draped fabric: straight lines might define the folds, while curved cross-hatching could depict the soft curves and wrinkles of the material. This variety in line quality keeps the drawing dynamic and prevents it from becoming static or monotonous.

Experiment with the spacing between your lines. Closely spaced lines create denser, darker values, while wider spacing results in lighter areas. This control over line spacing allows you to fine-tune the values within your drawing, achieving a greater sense of realism and depth. Consider drawing a tree trunk: dense cross-hatching could depict the rough bark, while looser lines could suggest the smoother areas.

Don't be afraid to break the rules. While a traditional approach to cross-hatching involves consistent angles and spacing, experimentation is encouraged. Try varying the pressure of your pen or brush to create lines that swell and taper. Experiment with different hatching patterns, such as curved or wavy lines, to create unique textures. Consider incorporating stippling or pointillism techniques within your cross-hatching to add further complexity.

Layering also allows you to work with different tools. You might start with a light pencil sketch to establish the basic forms, then layer over it with pen and ink. Alternatively, you could combine pen and brush, using the pen for fine details and the brush for broader washes of tone. This interplay of different media can create richly textured and visually engaging drawings. Imagine depicting a seashell: you could use fine pen lines to capture the intricate details of its surface, then layer over them with washes of diluted ink to suggest the subtle play of light and shadow.

Consider the direction of your lines. Lines that follow the contours of an object, known as contour lines, help define its form and volume. Lines that move against the form can create a sense of texture and movement. Experiment with different line directions to see how they impact the overall feeling of your drawing. Think of drawing a flowing river: lines that follow the curves of the water create a sense of smoothness and fluidity, while lines that move against the current could suggest ripples and turbulence.

Practicing cross-hatching and layering is crucial for developing your skills. Start with simple exercises, such as shading basic geometric shapes, then gradually move on to more complex subjects. Observe how light falls on different objects and try to replicate those effects using lines. As you gain confidence, experiment with different techniques and combinations of tools to discover your own unique style.

3.3 Implying Form and Volume

The power of line extends beyond mere contour; it can convincingly evoke three-dimensional form and volume on a flat surface. Think of line not as a simple outline, but as a descriptive tool capable of sculpting light and shadow, defining curves and planes, and creating the illusion of depth. This chapter will delve into specific techniques for achieving this, moving beyond the basics of line control to explore how we can make our drawings truly pop off the page.

One fundamental approach is to vary line weight and density to suggest the interplay of light and shadow. Imagine a sphere: the areas directly hit by light source will have thinner, lighter lines, while the areas receding into shadow will require thicker, denser lines. This gradual shift in line weight creates a smooth transition, mimicking the way light naturally falls on a curved surface. Practice this by drawing simple geometric forms like spheres, cubes, and cones, paying close attention to how light behaves on each shape. Use hatching and cross-hatching to build up tone and shadow, remembering that the density of your lines directly correlates to the depth of the shadow.

Contour lines, lines that follow the curves and edges of an object, play a crucial role in implying form. However, to truly capture volume, we must go beyond simple outlines. Consider incorporating cross-contour lines, which run perpendicular to the contour lines, wrapping around the form like the lines on a topographical map. These lines provide crucial information about the object's three-dimensionality, enhancing the illusion of depth and roundness. Experiment with different angles and curvatures for your cross-contour lines to fully capture the unique shape of your subject.

Another essential technique is understanding how light affects the appearance of form. Observe how light creates highlights and shadows on objects, and use your lines to replicate these effects. Highlights can be represented by areas of sparse or absent lines, allowing the white of the paper to shine through. Core shadows, the darkest areas on the object, will require dense hatching or cross-hatching. In between these extremes lie the halftones, areas of subtle gradation that connect the highlights and shadows, creating a seamless transition. Mastering the interplay of light and shadow is key to achieving convincing volume in your drawings.

Perspective further enhances the illusion of three-dimensionality. While a later chapter will delve deeper into perspective, it's important to consider how converging lines can create the impression of depth. As objects recede into space, they appear smaller and their lines converge towards a vanishing point. By incorporating these principles into your linework, you can create a more realistic sense of space and volume. Even without strict adherence to perspective rules, simply suggesting converging lines can significantly enhance the depth of your drawings.

Practice drawing objects from different angles and under varied lighting conditions. Try sketching simple still lifes, focusing on how light interacts with the various forms. Begin with basic shapes like fruits or vegetables, gradually progressing to more complex objects. Don't be afraid to experiment with different line weights, densities, and directions to discover what best captures the form and volume of your subject. Remember that drawing is a process of observation and interpretation. The more you practice, the more attuned you will become to the nuances of light and shadow, and the more effectively you will be able to use line to create the illusion of three-dimensional form.

Consider the negative space, the area around your subject, as an equally important element in defining form. The shape of the negative space directly relates to the shape of your subject, and by carefully defining this negative space with your lines, you can further enhance the perception of volume. Think of it as sculpting the air around the object, revealing its form through the surrounding emptiness.

Explore different hatching techniques to create varied textures and tonal effects. Parallel hatching, cross-hatching, and contour hatching can all be used to create different levels of depth and shadow. Vary the density and direction of your hatching lines to achieve a range of tonal values, from light to dark. Experiment with different pen nibs and brushstrokes to discover the unique qualities each offers in terms of line variation and texture.

Don't limit yourself to straight lines. Curved lines, swirling lines, and broken lines can all be used to create interesting and dynamic effects. Use curved lines to follow the contours of rounded objects and broken lines to suggest texture and detail. Explore the possibilities of combining different types of lines to achieve a greater range of expression.

Lastly, remember the importance of observation. Take the time to study the objects you are drawing, paying close attention to their shapes, textures, and how light interacts with them. The more closely you observe, the more accurately you will be able to represent form and volume in your drawings. Through consistent practice and experimentation, you will develop the ability to create drawings that not only depict objects but also evoke a tangible sense of their presence in space.

3.4 Perspective with Line

Understanding perspective is crucial for creating believable depth and space in your drawings. While traditional perspective relies on vanishing points and measured constructions, we'll explore how to achieve a sense of depth using solely the qualities of line itself – its weight, thickness, and direction. This approach offers a more intuitive and expressive way to portray three-dimensional space, especially useful when working with fluid, dynamic linework. Think of how a road appears to narrow as it stretches into the distance, or how the overlapping branches of a tree create a sense of depth. These are natural observations that we can translate directly into our drawing practice.

Consider the impact of line weight. A thicker, bolder line appears closer to the viewer, commanding attention and suggesting proximity. Conversely, a thinner, lighter line recedes, implying distance and creating a sense of airiness. By consciously varying the weight of your lines, you can control the viewer's eye, guiding them through the drawing and establishing a clear sense of foreground, middle ground, and background. Imagine drawing a row of trees. The trees in the foreground would be rendered with heavier, more detailed lines, while those further away would be drawn with lighter, simpler strokes.

Line direction plays an equally important role in conveying perspective. Converging lines, much like the aforementioned road example, naturally lead the eye towards a perceived vanishing point, even if it lies outside the frame of the drawing. This principle can be applied to a variety of subjects, from architectural structures to organic forms. Think of drawing a winding path through a forest. The curves of the path, combined with the converging lines of the surrounding trees, create a powerful sense of depth and direction.

Overlapping shapes are another powerful tool for suggesting depth. When one object partially obscures another, it immediately establishes a spatial relationship between them. The overlapping object is perceived as being in front, while the partially obscured object appears to be behind. This simple technique can be used to create complex layered compositions with a convincing sense of three-dimensionality. Imagine sketching a still life with overlapping fruits and vegetables. The overlaps instantly create a sense of depth and volume, making the composition feel more realistic.

Size variation also contributes to the illusion of perspective. Objects closer to the viewer appear larger, while those further away appear smaller. This is a fundamental principle of linear perspective, but it can be applied intuitively, without strict adherence to vanishing points. By varying the size of objects within your composition, you can create a sense of scale and distance, enhancing the overall sense of depth. Consider drawing a cityscape. The buildings in the foreground would be drawn larger and with more detail, while those in the distance would be smaller and less defined.

Atmospheric perspective, though often associated with color and value, can also be achieved with line. By using lighter, less detailed lines for distant objects, you can mimic the effect of atmospheric haze, creating a sense of distance and depth. This is particularly effective in landscapes, where the atmospheric perspective enhances the feeling of vastness and open space. Imagine drawing a mountain range. The peaks in the foreground would be drawn with darker, more defined lines, while the distant peaks would be rendered with lighter, hazier lines, suggesting atmospheric distance.

Combining these techniques allows you to create dynamic and expressive drawings with a convincing sense of depth and space. Experiment with different combinations of line weight, direction, overlap, size variation, and atmospheric perspective to discover what works best for you and your subject matter. Remember, the goal is not to create photorealistic representations but to capture the essence of the scene and convey it with fluidity and energy. Practice drawing everyday objects from different perspectives, focusing on how line can be used to create the illusion of depth.

Through careful manipulation of line, you can create drawings that not only capture the likeness of your subject but also evoke a sense of atmosphere and depth, drawing the viewer into your artistic vision. Remember to practice regularly, experimenting with different line qualities and techniques to develop your own personal style of perspective drawing. The more you explore, the more nuanced and expressive your work will become. This exploration is key to unlocking the full potential of line as a tool for creating dynamic and engaging artworks. Embrace the fluidity of line, and allow it to guide you in your journey of artistic discovery. By mastering the art of perspective with line, you'll not only enhance your drawing skills, but also deepen your understanding of how we perceive the three-dimensional world around us.

3.5 Dynamic Movement

Capturing movement on a static surface requires more than just depicting a subject in a particular pose. It demands an understanding of how to imbue your lines with the very essence of motion, creating a visual language that speaks of energy, momentum, and the passage of time. This involves a shift in perspective, moving from simply observing the outward appearance of a subject to capturing its underlying action and the forces that shape its movement. Think of a dancer mid-leap, a bird in flight, or a gust of wind rustling through leaves. These subjects are not static; they are defined by their dynamic energy.

To effectively convey dynamic movement, consider the use of directional lines. These lines, whether straight or curved, should follow the path and direction of the movement you are trying to depict. Imagine sketching a galloping horse. Your lines should not merely outline the horse's form but should actively describe the thrust of its legs, the arch of its back, and the flow of its mane as it surges forward. By aligning your lines with the direction of motion, you create a visual flow that guides the viewer's eye through the action.

Furthermore, explore the power of implied lines. These are lines that are not explicitly drawn but are suggested by the arrangement of other elements within the drawing. For instance, a series of converging lines can imply a vanishing point, creating a sense of depth and perspective that enhances the dynamism of a moving object. Similarly, the negative space around a subject can be used to suggest movement, as the empty areas define the shape and trajectory of the subject as it moves through space. Think of a fish swimming through water. The water itself is not drawn, but its presence and the fish's movement are implied by the shape of the fish and the flow of the surrounding negative space.

Varying the weight and pressure of your lines can further enhance the sense of movement. A thicker, heavier line can convey a sense of force or impact, while a lighter, thinner line can suggest grace and fluidity. For example, when drawing a bird in flight, use heavier lines to depict the downstroke of its wings, where the most power is exerted, and lighter lines for the upstroke, creating a visual contrast that emphasizes the dynamic interplay of forces. This variation in line weight not only adds visual interest but also contributes to a more nuanced and realistic portrayal of movement.

Rhythmic hatching, the technique of using closely spaced parallel lines to create tone and texture, also plays a vital role in depicting movement. By varying the direction, density, and curvature of your hatching lines, you can create a sense of flow and energy that follows the contours of your subject and emphasizes its motion. Imagine sketching a flowing drapery. The folds and ripples of the fabric can be beautifully rendered with rhythmic hatching, with the lines following the curves of the cloth and creating a sense of movement even in a static representation.

Consider the use of gestural lines. These quick, expressive lines capture the essential movement and energy of a subject without focusing on precise details. They are about capturing the feeling of motion, the overall sweep and direction of the action. Practice sketching quick gestures of moving figures or objects, focusing on the flow of the movement rather than the precise anatomical details. This practice will train your eye to see the essential lines of action and develop your ability to capture dynamic movement with economy and expressiveness.

Don't be afraid to exaggerate. Exaggerating certain aspects of a moving subject, such as the extension of a limb or the arc of a trajectory, can amplify the sense of movement and create a more dramatic and impactful image. Think of a superhero leaping across a building. Exaggerating the stretch of their body and the angle of their trajectory can enhance the sense of superhuman power and dynamic action.

Observation is key. Spend time observing moving subjects in the real world. Watch how people walk, run, and gesture. Observe the flight of birds, the movement of water, the swaying of trees in the wind. Pay attention to the rhythms, the patterns, the forces that shape their movements. The more you observe, the better you will become at understanding and capturing the essence of dynamic movement in your drawings. This careful observation will inform your linework, allowing you to create drawings that not only depict movement but also evoke the feeling and energy of the action itself. Remember, capturing dynamic movement is about more than simply replicating a pose; it's about capturing the life and energy within the motion.

4 Pen Techniques

Let's explore the fascinating world of stippling and pointillism. These techniques, relying on the meticulous placement of dots rather than continuous lines, offer a unique approach to building tone, texture, and form. Think of each dot as a tiny building block, contributing to a larger visual structure. With stippling, the density of dots creates the illusion of shading. Areas with tightly clustered dots appear darker, while sparsely dotted areas appear lighter. This gradual shift in dot density allows you to create subtle gradations of tone and achieve a remarkable level of detail. Pointillism, a more formalized version of stippling, employs distinct dots of pure color that optically mix when viewed from a distance. While we won't delve into color here, understanding the principle of pointillism can inform your approach to stippling with a pen. Consider how the varying proximity of your dots can create a sense of vibration and energy within the drawing.

Experiment with different pen nibs to vary the size and shape of your dots. A fine-nibbed pen will create delicate, precise dots perfect for intricate details and smooth transitions in tone. A broader nib, on the other hand, will produce larger, bolder dots, useful for creating textured surfaces and dramatic contrasts. Don't limit yourself to perfectly round dots either. Try tilting your pen to create elongated marks or experiment with different pressures to vary the dot's intensity. The key is to embrace the inherent textural qualities of stippling and pointillism, using the unique mark-making potential of each pen nib to your advantage.

Now, let's shift our focus to line variation exercises. Developing control over line weight and quality is crucial for creating dynamic and expressive drawings. Begin by practicing simple lines across the page. Vary the pressure as you draw, transitioning smoothly from thin, delicate lines to thick, bold strokes. Imagine your pen is a musical instrument, capable of producing a range of tones and dynamics. Just as a musician modulates their playing for emotional impact, you can modulate your line weight to create visual interest and convey a sense of depth.

Next, explore creating lines that taper from thick to thin or thin to thick. This exercise helps refine your control over pressure and teaches you to anticipate the line's evolution as you draw. Try drawing a series of curved lines, varying the weight along the curve to emphasize its form. Imagine drawing a ribbon twisting and turning in space. Thicker lines can represent areas where the ribbon is closer to the viewer, while thinner lines recede into the background. This interplay of line weight can imbue your drawings with a sense of three-dimensionality and movement.

Moving beyond individual lines, practice creating hatched areas. Hatching involves drawing a series of parallel lines to create tone and texture. Experiment with different line spacing, varying the density to achieve different levels of shading. Closely spaced lines will create a darker area, while wider spacing will appear lighter. Try cross-hatching, layering sets of parallel lines at different angles to further deepen the shadows and create richer textures. Consider the direction of your hatching lines as well. Hatching that follows the contours of an object can enhance its form and volume.

Another valuable exercise involves creating contour lines. Contour lines define the edges and surfaces of an object, capturing its three-dimensional form on a two-dimensional surface. Start by drawing simple objects like fruits or vegetables, carefully observing their shapes and contours. As you gain confidence, try drawing more complex objects, paying attention to the subtle shifts in plane and curvature. Remember, contour lines don't have to be perfectly continuous. Breaking the line or varying its weight can add expressiveness and capture the unique qualities of the subject.

Finally, explore blind contour drawing. In this exercise, you fix your gaze on the object you're drawing and move your pen across the paper without looking down. The goal isn't to create a perfect representation but rather to train your hand-eye coordination and develop a deeper understanding of form. Embrace the unexpected results. The often-distorted, whimsical lines produced through blind contour drawing can be surprisingly expressive and insightful, revealing a different way of seeing. By dedicating time to these exercises, you'll not only improve your pen control but also cultivate a more intuitive and expressive approach to linework.

4.1 Stippling & Pointillism

Let's dive into the fascinating world of stippling and pointillism, two techniques that rely on the meticulous placement of individual dots to create a complete image. While seemingly simple in concept, these methods offer a unique approach to building tone, texture, and form within a drawing, demanding patience and a keen eye for detail. They push you to think about your subject in terms of light and shadow, translating these observations into a series of carefully considered marks. This chapter will guide you through the nuances of each, offering practical tips and exercises to integrate these techniques into your artistic toolkit.

Stippling, at its core, involves using dots of varying sizes and densities to achieve different tonal values. A darker area is created by clustering dots closely together, while lighter areas are achieved by increasing the space between them. Think of it like a visual code, where density translates into darkness. The size of the dot also contributes to the overall effect. Larger dots naturally appear darker and can create a more textured surface, while smaller dots offer finer control and smoother gradations. Practice varying both dot size and spacing to achieve a wide range of tonal effects within your drawings. Try stippling a simple sphere, focusing on how the light source affects the placement and density of your dots.

Pointillism, while related to stippling, takes a more structured approach. Instead of simply varying dot size and density, pointillism utilizes distinct dots of pure color, placed strategically to create an optical illusion of blended colors when viewed from a distance. This technique was famously employed by Post-Impressionist painters like Georges Seurat and Paul Signac. While traditionally associated with painting, the principles of pointillism can be effectively applied to pen and ink drawing by using different colored inks or varying the intensity of black ink to simulate different hues. Experiment with applying pointillistic principles to a simple landscape, focusing on how different "colors" interact and blend visually.

Now, let's explore some practical exercises to refine your stippling and pointillism skills. Begin by practicing creating a smooth gradient from dark to light using only stippling. Pay close attention to the gradual shift in dot density and size. Once you feel comfortable with this, try creating a textured surface, like rough bark or a woven fabric, using stippling to convey the tactile qualities of the material. Challenge yourself to replicate the subtle nuances of light and shadow across the surface.

For pointillism practice, begin with a simple two-color exercise. Choose two contrasting ink colors or vary the intensity of your black ink. Create a small square divided in half, filling one side with one "color" and the other side with the second. Then, create a blended transition zone in the middle by intermingling the two colors using pointillistic technique. Observe how the colors appear to blend when viewed from a distance. Once comfortable, try creating a simple image using multiple "colors" and observe the interplay of light and shadow created by your dots.

Beyond these exercises, consider incorporating stippling and pointillism into your existing drawing practice. Perhaps use stippling to create a textured foreground in a landscape drawing, or employ pointillism to render a complex shadow. These techniques can be used in isolation or combined with other linework methods to add depth and interest to your art. Imagine using cross-hatching for the main structure of a subject and then employing stippling to add subtle tonal variations within the hatched areas. Or, perhaps use pointillism to create a vibrant background against which a more clearly defined subject stands out.

The beauty of stippling and pointillism lies in their versatility. They can be adapted to suit various subjects and styles, from realistic portrayals to more abstract interpretations. The key is to experiment, to find the approach that best aligns with your artistic vision. Don't be afraid to break the "rules" and explore the unique expressive possibilities these techniques offer. Practice, patience, and a willingness to explore are your greatest allies in mastering these intricate methods. Embrace the challenge and discover the power of the dot. It's a small mark with immense artistic potential.

4.2 Line Variation Exercises

Mastering line variation with a pen is akin to a musician mastering their instrument. It's about developing control, exploring nuances, and pushing the boundaries of what your tool can achieve. Think of your pen not just as a writing implement, but as an extension of your artistic vision. This chapter will guide you through focused exercises designed to expand your penmanship beyond the mundane and into the realm of dynamic, expressive linework. These exercises aren't about creating finished artworks, but about honing your skills and building a foundation for more complex pieces.

Begin by drawing a simple square. Now, fill that square with lines, but each line should be distinctly different. Vary the pressure as you draw. Start with a feather-light touch, barely kissing the paper, and gradually increase the pressure until the line becomes bold and saturated. Observe how the line thickens and thins, responding to the subtle shifts in your hand. Repeat this exercise with circles, triangles, and organic, freeform shapes. Focus on the feeling of the pen in your hand, the resistance of the paper, and the visual impact of each mark.

Next, explore the relationship between speed and line quality. Draw a series of horizontal lines across the page. Start with slow, deliberate strokes, paying close attention to the smoothness and consistency of each line. Gradually increase your speed, noticing how the lines become lighter, looser, and potentially more erratic. Introduce curves and loops into your practice, experimenting with how speed affects their fluidity and dynamism. Fast lines can convey energy and movement, while slow lines suggest stability and control.

Once you're comfortable with varying pressure and speed, combine these two elements. Draw a series of spirals, starting with a light, slow center and gradually increasing both pressure and speed as you move outwards. Imagine you're unwinding a coil of energy onto the page. Try the reverse, starting with a heavy, fast outer spiral and slowing down, lightening your touch as you move inwards. This exercise will help you develop a more intuitive understanding of how pressure and speed interact to create a wide range of line qualities.

Now let's introduce hatching, a fundamental technique for building tone and texture. Begin by filling a square with parallel lines, all drawn with consistent pressure and spacing. Then, create another square filled with cross-hatching, layering lines at different angles to create a denser, darker tone. Experiment with the distance between your lines, observing how closer spacing creates darker areas, while wider spacing allows more white paper to show through, resulting in lighter values. Try varying the pressure and speed within your hatching, creating a more dynamic and less mechanical effect.

Move beyond simple geometric shapes and apply these techniques to organic forms. Draw a simple fruit, like an apple or a pear. Use varying line weights and hatching to define its contours and create a sense of volume. Think about the direction of the light source and how it affects the shadows and highlights on the fruit's surface. Use lighter lines to depict the highlighted areas and heavier lines, combined with cross-hatching, to create the shadows. This exercise will help you understand how line can be used not just to outline an object, but to describe its three-dimensional form.

Finally, challenge yourself to create a composition using only lines. Choose a simple subject, such as a group of overlapping leaves or a seashell. Use all the techniques you've practiced – varying pressure, speed, hatching, and cross-hatching – to build up the image. Focus on creating a sense of depth and texture, using line to define the edges, contours, and surfaces of your subject. Don't be afraid to experiment and push your boundaries. The goal here is not to create a perfect representation, but to explore the expressive possibilities of line and develop your own unique style. Remember, each line you draw is a step towards greater mastery of this versatile and powerful medium.

5 Brush Techniques

Holding a brush offers a unique dynamism compared to a pen. The range of marks you can achieve, from delicate washes to bold, textured strokes, opens up exciting possibilities for your artwork. Think of the brush as an extension of your hand, capable of whispering or shouting across the paper. This chapter explores the core brush techniques that will allow you to control this powerful tool and harness its expressive potential.

Let's start with the fundamental brushstrokes. A flat brush, held at different angles, can create a variety of marks. Held perpendicular to the paper, it produces a broad, even stroke, perfect for laying down washes of color or ink. Angling the brush creates a thinner, more tapered stroke, ideal for defining edges or adding fine details. Experiment with varying the pressure as you move the brush across the paper. A light touch yields a delicate, almost translucent line, while increasing pressure creates a bolder, more saturated mark. Practice these basic strokes until they become second nature. Try creating a series of graded washes, transitioning smoothly from dark to light. This exercise will familiarize you with controlling the ink flow and pressure.

Moving on from basic strokes, we delve into the world of washes. Washes are diluted applications of ink or watercolor, creating a transparent layer of color. They can be used to establish a base tone, build up subtle gradations of value, or suggest atmospheric depth. To create a wash, dilute your ink or watercolor with water, experimenting with different ratios to achieve the desired intensity. Apply the wash evenly across your paper, using a large, flat brush. For a graded wash, start with a concentrated application of color and gradually dilute it with water as you work your way down the paper. Controlling the moisture content of both your brush and the paper is crucial for achieving smooth, even washes.

Dry brush technique offers a completely different textural experience. Instead of loading the brush with ink or paint, you blot most of it away, leaving the bristles relatively dry. When dragged across the paper, the dry brush creates a broken, scratchy texture, perfect for suggesting rough surfaces, foliage, or weathered materials. The key to dry brushing is to experiment with different levels of dryness. A slightly damp brush will produce a softer, more subtle texture, while a very dry brush creates a more pronounced, almost splintered effect. Try using a stiff-bristled brush for a more dramatic dry brush effect.

Now, let's consider the exciting interplay between pen and brush. Combining these two tools allows you to create artwork with remarkable depth and complexity. You might use fine pen lines to define the contours of an object and then apply washes of color with a brush to create depth and shadow. Alternatively, you could use dry brush techniques to build up texture and then overlay precise details with a pen. The possibilities are endless. Consider a landscape drawing. You might use a pen to sketch the outline of trees and rocks, then use a brush to add washes of color for the sky and water. Finally, you could return to the pen to add finer details, like the texture of bark or the ripples on the water's surface.

Expressive mark-making lies at the heart of dynamic drawing. It's about using your tools in a way that conveys emotion, movement, and energy. Don't be afraid to experiment with unconventional brushstrokes, unexpected angles, and varying pressures. Let your hand move freely across the paper, guided by your intuition. Try using the side of the brush to create sweeping, gestural marks, or dabbing the tip to create a series of dots or dashes. Think about the feeling you want to convey in your drawing and let your brushstrokes reflect that emotion.

Finally, let's explore how brush techniques can be used to create depth and shadow. Washes are particularly effective for this purpose. By layering washes of varying intensities, you can create a sense of volume and recession. Darker washes can be used to depict areas of shadow, while lighter washes suggest highlights and illuminated surfaces. Dry brush techniques can also be used to enhance the illusion of depth. By applying dry brush strokes in a directional manner, you can create a sense of form and texture, adding to the overall three-dimensionality of your drawing. Remember to consider your light source and how it affects the shadows and highlights within your composition. Practice these techniques by drawing simple objects like spheres and cubes, focusing on how light interacts with their surfaces. As you gain confidence, you can apply these principles to more complex subjects.

5.1 Brushstrokes and Washes

Holding a brush offers a different kind of intimacy with your drawing surface compared to a pen. The softness of the bristles, their responsiveness to pressure and angle, allows for a unique range of marks, from delicate whispers to bold pronouncements. Explore the basic brushstrokes first: the flat stroke, achieved by pressing the belly of the brush onto the paper, creates broad, even washes of color. The angled stroke, made by using just the tip or edge of the brush, produces fine lines ideal for details and delicate textures. Practice transitioning smoothly between thick and thin strokes within a single gesture, varying the pressure as you move the brush across the paper. This control is crucial for imbuing your lines with dynamism and character. Don't be afraid to experiment with different brush sizes and shapes; each offers its own expressive potential. A round brush, for example, is versatile for both fine lines and broader strokes, while a flat brush excels at creating sharp edges and geometric shapes.

Washes are another fundamental technique in brushwork, allowing for the creation of smooth gradients and atmospheric effects. Dilute your ink or paint with water to achieve the desired transparency. Load your brush generously with the diluted mixture and apply it evenly to the paper, working quickly to prevent hard edges from forming. Experiment with layering washes, allowing each layer to dry partially before applying the next. This technique creates subtle variations in tone and depth, enriching the visual complexity of your work.

Try tilting your drawing surface to encourage the wash to flow in specific directions, creating interesting gradations and organic shapes. This method is particularly effective for depicting skies, water, and other fluid forms.

Think of the brush as an extension of your hand, a tool that translates your thoughts and emotions directly onto the page. Don't be constrained by the idea of perfect lines or precise forms. Embrace the unpredictable nature of the medium, allowing for happy accidents and spontaneous marks. The beauty of brushwork often lies in its imperfections, the subtle variations in tone and texture that give a drawing its unique character. Explore different brush handling techniques – twisting, dabbing, dragging – to discover the full range of expressive possibilities.

Consider the paper you're working on as an active participant in the process. Different paper textures interact with the brush in unique ways. A smooth, hot-pressed paper allows for crisp, clean lines and even washes, while a rougher, cold-pressed paper adds texture and a degree of unpredictability to your brushstrokes. Experiment with various paper types to discover which best suits your style and subject matter. The absorbency of the paper also plays a significant role. Highly absorbent paper will create softer, diffused edges, while less absorbent paper will maintain sharper lines and more vibrant colors.

Observe the world around you with a heightened awareness of light and shadow, form and texture. Translate these observations into your brushwork, using washes and varying brushstrokes to capture the essence of what you see. Practice depicting different textures, such as the roughness of bark, the smoothness of a petal, or the fluffiness of clouds. Pay attention to the way light interacts with these surfaces, creating highlights and shadows that define their form. Use your brush to capture these nuances, building up layers of washes and strokes to achieve a sense of depth and dimension.

The rhythm of your brushstrokes can also contribute to the overall mood and energy of your drawing. Quick, energetic strokes convey movement and dynamism, while slow, deliberate strokes suggest calmness and stillness. Vary your pace to create visual interest and reflect the emotional content of your work. Practice drawing from life, focusing on capturing the essence of your subject through expressive brushwork. Don't get bogged down in details; instead, strive to convey the overall feeling and movement of the scene.

When working with washes, consider the impact of color on the overall composition. Even with monochromatic inks, subtle variations in value can be achieved by layering washes or diluting the ink to different degrees. Experiment with color mixing if you're using paints, observing how different hues interact and create new shades. The interplay of colors can add depth and complexity to your washes, enhancing the emotional impact of your work. Don't be afraid to push the boundaries of traditional techniques, experimenting with unconventional color combinations and layering methods.

Remember that mastering brush techniques takes time and practice. Embrace the learning process, allowing yourself to make mistakes and learn from them. Experiment with different brushes, inks, papers, and techniques to discover what works best for you. Develop your own unique approach to brushwork, allowing your personal style to emerge through exploration and experimentation. With dedication and patience, you'll unlock the expressive potential of the brush, transforming simple lines and washes into dynamic and captivating works of art.

5.2 Dry Brush Effects

The dry brush technique offers a unique approach to creating texture and depth in your artwork. Unlike traditional brushwork that relies on a fully loaded brush and smooth application, the dry brush technique involves using a brush with very little moisture, resulting in a broken, scratchy line. This creates a distinctive visual effect, adding a sense of roughness, age, or texture to your drawings, perfect for depicting weathered surfaces, foliage, or animal fur. Think of it as whispering with your brush instead of speaking.

Start by selecting an appropriate brush. A stiffer brush, like a bristle brush or even an old, slightly frayed brush, works best for dry brushing. The stiffness allows for more control over the broken line effect. Softer brushes tend to deposit more pigment, counteracting the intended effect. Experiment with various brush shapes and sizes to discover which best suits your style and the specific texture you're trying to achieve. A flat brush will create broader, more consistent dry brush strokes, while a round brush allows for finer details and variations in line weight.

Prepare your brush by loading it with a small amount of ink or paint. Remove almost all of the excess by wiping the brush on a clean cloth or piece of paper.

The goal is to have just enough pigment on the brush to create a faint, broken line when dragged across the paper. Too much moisture will result in a solid stroke, negating the dry brush effect. This delicate balance between too much and too little moisture is crucial to mastering the technique.

Now, apply the brush to your paper using light pressure. Drag the brush across the surface, allowing the texture of the paper to break up the line. The drier the brush, the more broken and textured the line will appear. Experiment with different angles and pressures to achieve a variety of effects. A light touch and shallow angle will create a subtle texture, while a heavier hand and steeper angle will result in a more pronounced, scratchy line.

The dry brush technique thrives on experimentation. Vary your brushstrokes. Try short, choppy strokes for a rough, uneven texture, or long, sweeping strokes for a more directional, weathered appearance. Consider the direction of your strokes. Following the contours of an object will enhance its form, while cross-hatching with dry brush strokes can create a sense of depth and volume.

The beauty of dry brushing lies in its versatility. It can be used to suggest a wide range of textures, from the delicate fuzz of a peach to the coarse bark of a tree. Consider using dry brushing to depict weathered wood, rocky terrain, or the rusting surface of metal. In portraiture, dry brushing can be used to create the subtle texture of hair or wrinkles. By varying your brushstrokes and pressure, you can achieve a remarkable degree of realism and depth.

Explore the possibilities of layering dry brush strokes. Applying multiple layers with different colors or tones can create a richer, more complex texture. For instance, you could start with a light layer of gray to establish the base texture, followed by a layer of brown to add warmth and depth. Experiment with different color combinations to see how they interact and contribute to the overall effect.

Dry brushing can also be effectively combined with other techniques. Try layering dry brush strokes over washes for a unique textural effect. The dry brush will pick up the underlying wash color, creating subtle variations and adding depth to the washed area. Conversely, applying a wash over dry brush strokes can soften the harshness of the dry brush lines, creating a more blended and integrated appearance.

Consider the type of paper you are using. A rougher paper surface, such as cold-pressed watercolor paper, will amplify the dry brush effect, creating more pronounced textures. A smoother paper, like hot-pressed watercolor paper, will result in a less broken line, offering a different kind of subtle texture. Experiment with various paper types to discover which best suits your style and the specific effect you're aiming for.

Don't be afraid to experiment with different media as well. While ink and watercolor are commonly used for dry brushing, you can also try acrylic paints, gouache, or even colored pencils. Each medium will react differently with the dry brush technique, offering unique textures and possibilities. This experimentation is key to developing your own unique style and expanding your artistic repertoire.

Finally, practice and observation are essential to mastering the dry brush technique. Observe the textures around you, paying attention to the subtle nuances and variations in surface quality. Practice replicating these textures using dry brushing, experimenting with different brushstrokes, pressures, and colors. With patience and persistence, you'll develop a keen eye for texture and the ability to capture it effectively using this versatile and expressive technique.

5.3 Combining Pen & Brush

The marriage of pen and brush offers a rich tapestry of possibilities for the artist seeking dynamic and expressive linework. Each tool possesses unique strengths, and their combined use can lead to artwork with incredible depth, texture, and visual interest. Think of the pen as the architect, providing structure and detail, while the brush acts as the painter, washing in atmosphere and broad strokes of tone. This chapter will explore how to effectively weave these two distinct voices together, creating a harmonious and captivating visual narrative.

Begin by considering the role each tool will play in your drawing. Will the pen establish the foundational sketch, with the brush adding washes of color and texture? Or perhaps the brush will lay down initial shapes and values, allowing the pen to refine details and add crisp lines. Experiment with different approaches to discover what best suits your subject and artistic vision. Don't be afraid to let the tools inform the process. Sometimes, the unexpected interplay between pen and brush can lead to exciting discoveries.

Imagine sketching a bustling cityscape. You might use a fine-liner pen to meticulously render the architectural details – the sharp edges of buildings, the intricate patterns of windows, the delicate tracery of fire escapes. Then, switch to a brush loaded with diluted ink to suggest the soft glow of streetlights, the hazy atmosphere of a rainy day, or the bustling energy of crowds moving through the streets. The contrast between the precise pen lines and the fluid brushstrokes creates a dynamic tension, capturing the essence of the urban environment.

Another approach involves using the brush to establish broad areas of tone and texture. Consider a portrait. A soft brush loaded with a light wash can define the planes of the face, creating subtle gradations of light and shadow. Then, a pen can be used to add details – the curve of an eyebrow, the glint in an eye, the texture of hair. This technique allows you to build up the image gradually, layering lines and washes to achieve a rich and nuanced effect.

Explore the expressive potential of dry brush techniques in combination with pen. Imagine depicting a windswept landscape. A dry brush dragged across the paper can create the textured appearance of grasses swaying in the breeze. Then, use a pen to add details – the stark outline of a distant tree, the jagged edges of rocks, the delicate lines of a fence. The contrast between the rough texture of the dry brush and the precise lines of the pen evokes a sense of movement and atmosphere.

Don't limit yourself to black ink. Experiment with different colors and inks to further enhance the visual richness of your combined pen and brush drawings. A sepia ink wash applied with a brush can create a warm, antique feel, while a vibrant blue ink used with a pen can add a touch of unexpected color and energy. Consider the emotional impact of different colors and how they can contribute to the overall mood and message of your artwork.

Practice different types of hatching and cross-hatching with both pen and brush. A fine-liner pen can create dense, tightly woven hatching that builds up deep shadows. A brush, on the other hand, can be used to create more gestural and expressive hatching, adding a sense of movement and energy to the drawing. Explore how combining these different hatching styles can create a greater range of tonal values and textures.

Pay close attention to the interplay between positive and negative space. The white of the paper can be just as important as the lines and washes you create. Use the pen to define shapes and contours, and the brush to create areas of wash that suggest depth and atmosphere. Think about how the negative space interacts with the positive elements to create a balanced and harmonious composition.

Remember that the key to successful combining of pen and brush lies in understanding the unique characteristics of each tool and exploring their expressive potential in concert. Embrace experimentation, be open to unexpected results, and allow the interplay of these two dynamic tools to enrich your artistic journey. Through practice and exploration, you will develop a deeper understanding of how pen and brush can work together to create truly captivating and dynamic drawings. Let the fluidity of the line guide your hand, and the rhythm of the hatching breathe life into your artwork.

5.4 Expressive Mark-Making

True mastery of line goes beyond technical proficiency; it lies in imbuing each stroke with intention and expressiveness. This chapter explores mark-making with brush and pen, not simply as tools for representation, but as instruments for conveying emotion, energy, and a unique artistic vision. Think of your tools as extensions of your own gestural language, capable of whispering subtleties or shouting pronouncements across the page. This shift in perspective, from mere depiction to expressive communication, opens a world of possibilities within your linework.

Consider the humble dot. Made with the delicate tip of a fine-liner pen, it can represent a pinpoint of light, a distant star. Pressed firmly with a broad-nibbed pen, that same dot becomes a bold statement, a punctuation mark in the visual narrative. Multiply these dots, vary their density and pressure, and suddenly you're crafting textures, suggesting shadows, even implying form. This is the power of expressive mark-making: transforming simple strokes into complex visual experiences. With a brush, the dot expands into a dab, a splash, a pool of pigment. Each carries its own weight, its own personality.

Explore the expressive potential of different marks beyond the dot. A jagged, staccato line can convey tension, a sense of unease. A smooth, flowing curve breathes elegance and grace into a composition. Short, rapid strokes pulsate with energy, while long, deliberate lines evoke a sense of calm. Vary the pressure of your brush or pen as you move across the page. A light touch produces a delicate whisper of a line, while a heavier hand yields a bold, decisive mark. This variation in line weight is crucial for creating visual interest and depth. Experiment with different tools to expand your mark-making vocabulary. A stiff-bristled brush creates a dry, scratchy texture, perfect for depicting weathered surfaces or suggesting the roughness of bark. A soft, supple brush allows for smooth gradations of tone and fluid, expressive gestures. Switch between pen nibs to discover the distinct personality of each. A flexible nib responds to pressure, producing lines that swell and taper, while a rigid nib offers consistent precision. Try rotating your pen or brush as you draw, creating calligraphic effects and dynamic variations in line width.

Don't be afraid to break free from traditional drawing techniques. Explore unconventional methods of mark-making. Drag the side of your pen across the paper to create broad, textured strokes. Flick your wrist to create splatters of ink that add an element of spontaneity and energy to your work. Use the end of a paintbrush handle to scratch lines into wet ink or paint, revealing the layers beneath. Embrace accidents and unexpected results; they often lead to exciting discoveries and new avenues of expression. These seemingly random marks can inject life and spontaneity into your drawings, adding a layer of visual intrigue.

Think about the rhythm of your marks. Just as a musician varies the tempo and dynamics of a musical piece, you can vary the pacing and intensity of your strokes. A series of rapid, closely spaced lines creates a sense of urgency and movement, while slow, deliberate marks convey a sense of calmness and contemplation. Consider the negative space around your marks. The empty areas of your drawing are just as important as the marks themselves. They provide breathing room, allowing the eye to move comfortably through the composition. They can also contribute to the overall feeling of the piece, suggesting vastness, emptiness, or quiet contemplation. Don't overcrowd your drawings. Leave room for the white of the paper to breathe and interact with your marks. Practice these techniques regularly, not with the goal of creating finished masterpieces, but with the intention of exploring the expressive possibilities of your tools. Fill sketchbooks with experiments, allowing yourself the freedom to play and discover new ways of making marks. Over time, these experiments will become ingrained in your artistic vocabulary, allowing you to communicate your ideas and emotions with greater nuance and expressiveness. Remember, expressive mark-making is not about achieving perfection; it's about finding your own unique voice and allowing it to resonate through your lines.

5.5 Creating Depth and Shadow

Understanding how to manipulate light and shadow with pen and brush is crucial for creating convincing three-dimensional forms on a two-dimensional surface. This isn't simply about shading dark areas; it's about understanding how light interacts with objects, creating highlights, mid-tones, core shadows, cast shadows, and reflected light. Mastering these elements will elevate your drawings from flat representations to dynamic and engaging works of art. This chapter delves into specific techniques for achieving depth and shadow using both pen and brush, enabling you to add a captivating realism to your artwork. We'll explore how varying line weight, ink washes, and strategic hatching can transform your drawings.

Consider the direction and intensity of your light source. A single, strong light source creates high contrast between light and shadow, resulting in dramatic and well-defined forms. Diffused light, on the other hand, softens shadows and reduces contrast, leading to a more subtle and atmospheric effect. Observe how light falls on simple objects like spheres, cubes, and cylinders. Notice how the highlights, mid-tones, and shadows transition across the surfaces, defining their curves and planes. Replicating these gradations of light and shadow in your drawings is key to achieving a sense of volume.

With pen work, achieving depth and shadow relies heavily on line control and hatching techniques. Varying the weight and density of your lines allows you to create the illusion of light and shadow. Denser, thicker lines recede, while lighter, thinner lines advance. Cross-hatching, layering lines at different angles, allows you to build up tone gradually, creating a sense of depth and volume. Experiment with different hatching patterns, from tight, closely spaced lines for darker areas to looser, more open hatching for lighter tones. Pay attention to the direction of your hatching; it should follow the contours of the form, enhancing the three-dimensional illusion. Stippling, a technique using dots to create tone, can also be used effectively to suggest shadow and texture, adding another layer of visual interest to your work.

Brush techniques offer a different approach to creating depth and shadow.

Washes, diluted ink applied with a brush, allow you to create smooth gradations of tone, perfect for depicting soft shadows and subtle transitions between light and dark. Vary the concentration of your ink to control the intensity of the wash. Layering washes, allowing each layer to dry before applying the next, builds up depth and complexity. Dry brush, a technique where a brush loaded with minimal ink is dragged across the paper, creates a textured, broken effect ideal for depicting rough surfaces and adding depth to shadowed areas.

Combining pen and brush offers the most versatile approach. You can use pen to establish the initial structure and details of your subject, then use brush washes to add shadows and create a sense of atmosphere. The contrast between the precise lines of the pen and the fluid washes of the brush can create a dynamic and visually engaging piece. Imagine sketching a portrait with pen, capturing the likeness and features with fine lines. Then, using a brush, wash in soft shadows around the eyes, nose, and mouth to create depth and dimension. Highlights can be subtly suggested by leaving areas of the paper untouched.

Practice creating a series of tonal scales, transitioning from light to dark, using both pen and brush. This will help you develop a sensitivity to tonal variations and improve your ability to control the medium. Experiment with different pen nibs and brush types to explore the range of effects achievable. Don't be afraid to make mistakes; experimentation is a crucial part of the learning process. By combining careful observation with practiced technique, you'll master the art of creating depth and shadow, bringing your drawings to life with a compelling sense of realism and artistry. Remember to practice regularly, observing light and shadow in the world around you.

6 Putting It All Together

Now comes the moment to synthesize everything you've learned. Consider this chapter a bridge, connecting the individual techniques you've practiced to the creation of complete, compelling artworks. It's where the technical skills transform into artistic expression, where you move from practicing scales to composing your own symphony of lines. This process involves two key aspects: understanding compositional principles and cultivating your unique artistic voice.

Composition is the language of visual art. It dictates how the elements within your drawing interact with each other and the overall space. Think of the page as a stage and your lines, textures, and washes as the performers. A well-composed drawing guides the viewer's eye through the scene, creating a sense of harmony and balance. Start by considering the rule of thirds – a guideline suggesting that placing key elements off-center often creates more dynamic and engaging compositions. Imagine a grid dividing your paper into nine equal sections. The intersections of these lines are powerful focal points. Try positioning the primary subject of your drawing near one of these intersections. Another crucial aspect is negative space – the area around and between the objects you draw. Don't underestimate its power. Negative space is not simply emptiness; it's an active participant in the composition, shaping the perceived form and contributing to the overall balance. Experiment with varying the amount of negative space to see how it affects the feeling of your piece. Sometimes, less is truly more.

Balance, a close relative of composition, concerns the visual weight distribution within your drawing. Symmetrical balance creates a sense of formality and stability, while asymmetrical balance, where visual weight is distributed unevenly, can be more dynamic and expressive. Achieving balance isn't about achieving perfect symmetry or asymmetry; it's about creating a feeling of equilibrium that feels right for the specific drawing. Consider the visual weight of your lines, textures, and areas of light and shadow. Darker areas tend to feel heavier than lighter areas, complex textures heavier than smooth ones. Use these differences to create a balanced composition that holds the viewer's attention. Imagine balancing a seesaw, adjusting the weight on either side until it rests evenly.

Moving beyond the technical aspects of composition, the next step in bringing everything together is to discover and nurture your unique artistic style. This is the process of finding your artistic voice, the distinct way you express yourself through your art. It's where your personality, experiences, and perspectives shine through. Think of the artists you admire. What draws you to their work? Is it their bold use of line, their delicate washes, or the way they capture emotion? Analyzing the work of others can help you identify the qualities you appreciate and want to incorporate into your own style. However, remember that inspiration is different from imitation. Your goal is not to copy another artist's style, but to learn from them and synthesize those lessons with your own unique vision.

Experimentation is crucial in this journey. Don't be afraid to push the boundaries of what you've learned. Try combining pen and brush in unexpected ways. Explore different papers, inks, and even unconventional tools. Play with different compositional approaches, pushing the limits of balance and negative space. Every experiment, successful or not, is a step toward refining your artistic voice. Each mark you make, each wash you apply, adds another layer to your artistic vocabulary. Embrace the process of discovery. There's no right or wrong answer in this exploration. The journey itself is the reward. As you continue to practice and experiment, you'll find that certain techniques and approaches resonate more strongly with you than others. These preferences are the building blocks of your style. Embrace them. They're what make your work uniquely yours.

Developing a personal style isn't a destination but a continuous journey. It's a process of constant refinement, influenced by your experiences, inspirations, and ongoing exploration. It's the culmination of all the techniques you've learned, filtered through the lens of your individual perspective. As you progress, you'll find that your style evolves organically, deepening and maturing with each new drawing you create. Don't be afraid to let your style change and grow over time. Embrace the evolution. It's a testament to your artistic growth and the ongoing conversation you're having with your art. Trust your instincts, embrace the process, and allow your unique artistic voice to emerge.

6.1 Composition & Balance

A strong composition is the bedrock of any successful artwork. It guides the viewer's eye, creates a sense of harmony, and ultimately delivers the artist's intended message. Think of composition as the underlying architecture of your drawing, the framework upon which all your carefully rendered lines and brushstrokes rest. Without a solid compositional foundation, even the most technically proficient linework can fall flat. Balance is the cornerstone of this framework, distributing visual weight evenly across the piece. This doesn't necessarily mean perfect symmetry; rather, it's about creating a sense of equilibrium that feels both dynamic and resolved.

Consider the format of your drawing – portrait, landscape, or square – and how that shape interacts with the subject matter. A sweeping landscape might lend itself to a horizontal format, while a portrait might benefit from a vertical orientation. This initial decision influences how you arrange elements within the frame. Begin by identifying the focal point, the area you want the viewer's eye to be drawn to first. This could be a specific object, a concentration of detail, or a point of high contrast. Once established, build your composition around this central anchor.

The rule of thirds is a helpful guideline for positioning your focal point. Imagine dividing your drawing into thirds both horizontally and vertically, creating nine equal sections. Placing your focal point at or near the intersection of these lines often results in a more engaging and dynamic composition. Avoid placing your focal point dead center, as this can create a static, less interesting image. Similarly, be mindful of negative space, the areas around and between the objects in your drawing. Negative space is just as important as the positive space occupied by your subject; it provides breathing room and helps define the shapes within your composition.

Now, think about the visual pathways you want the viewer's eye to follow. Leading lines, created by roads, fences, or even the direction of a gaze, can draw the eye into the scene and towards the focal point. Curves and diagonals add dynamism and energy, while horizontal and vertical lines create stability and calm. Use a combination of these to create a sense of visual rhythm and flow. Imagine how a viewer's eye might wander across your piece; are they guided smoothly through the scene, or do they get stuck in certain areas?

Balance in composition involves more than just positioning elements. It also encompasses the distribution of light and dark, texture and detail, and even the types of lines you use. A heavily detailed area can be balanced by a simpler, more open space. Similarly, a dark area can be offset by a lighter one. Consider the interplay of these elements as you build your composition. Just as a musician balances different instruments in an orchestra, you need to balance the various visual elements in your drawing to create a harmonious whole.

Experiment with different compositional arrangements. Thumbnail sketches are a valuable tool for this, allowing you to quickly explore various options before committing to a final design. These small, quick studies can help you determine the most effective placement of elements, the best use of negative space, and the overall balance of your composition. Don't be afraid to break the rules once you understand them. While guidelines like the rule of thirds can be helpful starting points, they aren't hard and fast rules. Sometimes, breaking the rules can lead to the most unexpected and compelling results.

Finally, remember that composition is not a purely intellectual exercise. It's about feeling and intuition as much as it is about technical principles. Step back from your work regularly and assess it with fresh eyes. Does it feel balanced? Does it draw your eye in and hold your attention? Trust your instincts and be willing to make adjustments as needed. Developing a strong sense of composition takes time and practice, but it's a crucial skill for any artist striving to create compelling and dynamic drawings. Through careful consideration of balance, visual pathways, and the interplay of elements, you can elevate your linework from simple marks on a page to powerful visual statements.

6.2 Finding Your Style

Style isn't something you find like a lost key. It's cultivated, a slow burn built upon exploration, practice, and a deep understanding of your own creative impulses. Think of it as a conversation between you and your tools, a dialogue whispered through the lines on the page. This chapter, then, isn't about giving you a style. It's about giving you the tools to unearth your own. Begin by revisiting the exercises from previous chapters. Don't simply repeat them, but actively analyze which techniques resonated most strongly with you. Were you drawn to the delicate intricacies of stippling, or the bold, sweeping strokes of the brush? Did you find yourself gravitating towards intricate cross-hatching, or the loose, expressive energy of gestural lines? Recognizing these preferences is the first step towards defining your artistic voice.

Consider your subject matter. What are you drawn to depict? Do you find beauty in the natural world, the rigid geometry of urban landscapes, or the expressive contours of the human form? Your subject matter inherently influences your style. The flowing lines used to capture the movement of a bird in flight will differ drastically from the precise, controlled lines used to render the architectural details of a building. This interplay between subject and style is a crucial element of your artistic development. Experiment with applying the techniques you enjoyed to subjects that inspire you. See how your preferred methods adapt and evolve when applied to different forms and textures.

Now, think about the artists whose work you admire. Whose lines sing to you? Whose compositions make you catch your breath? Analyzing the work of others, dissecting their techniques and stylistic choices, can provide invaluable insights into your own preferences. Don't aim to copy their style; instead, try to understand what resonates with you about their work. Is it their use of light and shadow, their dynamic compositions, or their unique approach to line weight and texture? Identifying these elements can help you articulate what you strive for in your own art. Create a mood board, either physically or digitally, collecting images of artwork that inspires you. Study the common threads that run through these pieces. What are the recurring themes, techniques, or stylistic choices? This exercise can help you identify the underlying principles that draw you to certain styles, providing a clearer understanding of your own aesthetic inclinations.

Reflect on your own personality. Are you meticulous and detail-oriented, or bold and spontaneous? Your inherent personality traits often manifest in your artistic style. A patient, detail-oriented individual might naturally gravitate towards intricate penwork and meticulous rendering, while a more free-spirited individual might prefer the loose, expressive qualities of brushwork. Allow your personality to inform your linework. If you're naturally energetic and expressive, don't be afraid to let that energy flow through your lines. Conversely, if you're more introspective and detail-oriented, embrace the precision and control that your nature allows.

Experiment with different tools and materials. The choice between a fine-tipped pen and a broad brush, a smooth sheet of paper and a textured surface, all contribute to the overall aesthetic of your work. Explore a range of options, pushing beyond your comfort zone to discover new possibilities. Try using different inks, experimenting with varying levels of opacity and viscosity. Explore different paper textures, from smooth Bristol board to rough watercolor paper. Each combination of tools and materials will yield a unique result, further shaping your individual style. Don't limit yourself to traditional drawing tools. Experiment with unconventional materials like twigs, sponges, or even your fingers to apply ink or paint. These unexpected approaches can lead to surprising and unique results, further pushing the boundaries of your stylistic explorations.

Finally, and perhaps most importantly, be patient. Developing a distinct artistic style is a journey, not a destination. Embrace the process of experimentation, allow yourself to make mistakes, and don't be afraid to deviate from the prescribed path. Your style will evolve over time, shaped by your experiences, influences, and ongoing exploration. The more you practice, the more refined and distinctive your style will become. It's the accumulation of these explorations, the gradual refinement of your technique, and the deepening understanding of your own artistic voice that will ultimately define your unique style.

7 Beyond the Basics

Now that you've established a solid foundation in line control, pen and brush techniques, let's venture beyond the structured exercises and delve into the realm of uninhibited exploration. This is where true artistic growth blossoms, where you shed the constraints of learned techniques and allow your intuition to guide your hand. Experimentation is not about discarding what you've learned, but rather about integrating those skills into a more personal and expressive visual language. Consider it a playground where you can bend the rules, push boundaries, and discover unexpected possibilities within the simple elegance of line.

Think of renowned artists like Vincent van Gogh, whose energetic brushstrokes pulsed with emotion, or Aubrey Beardsley, whose intricate pen lines danced with a delicate, decorative quality. These artists didn't simply master the technical aspects of their chosen media; they imbued their work with a distinctive personality. They explored, they experimented, and they weren't afraid to break away from conventional approaches. This is the spirit we want to cultivate. Take the cross-hatching technique you've learned, for instance. Instead of using uniform, parallel lines, try varying their density, direction, and curvature. Overlap them in unexpected ways. See what happens when you combine cross-hatching with stippling or washes, blending the textures and tones to create a richer visual experience.

Don't be afraid to embrace the unexpected. Accidents, so-called mistakes, can often lead to the most exciting discoveries. A stray ink blot can become the nucleus of a new composition. A jagged, uncontrolled line can spark an unexpected sense of dynamism. These unplanned moments often hold a raw energy and authenticity that can be difficult to achieve through deliberate planning. Embrace the unpredictable nature of ink and paint. Let the materials themselves guide you, suggesting new pathways and possibilities. Try working on different surfaces: textured paper, wood, even fabric. The interaction between the medium and the surface can create fascinating and unpredictable results, enriching your visual vocabulary.

Developing a personal voice is a journey, not a destination. It's about continually exploring, questioning, and refining your approach. Look for inspiration beyond the traditional art world. Study the natural world, observing the intricate patterns in leaves, the delicate lines of a spider's web, the rhythmic flow of water. Find inspiration in calligraphy, graphic design, even music. Let these diverse influences permeate your work, shaping your unique style. Keep a sketchbook handy at all times. Fill it with quick studies, experimental mark-making, and fleeting thoughts. This isn't about creating finished pieces; it's about nurturing a constant dialogue with your materials and ideas. It's a space for free association, a visual journal where you can explore without judgment.

Consider your sketchbook a testing ground for new techniques and approaches. Try different pens, brushes, and inks. Experiment with varying paper weights and textures. Document your process, noting what works, what doesn't, and what sparks your curiosity. Over time, patterns will emerge. You'll discover certain techniques, subjects, or approaches that resonate with you more deeply. These are the seeds of your artistic voice. Nurture them. Allow them to grow and evolve organically.

Engage with other artists. Join a local drawing group, attend workshops, or connect with artists online. Sharing your work and receiving feedback can be invaluable. It can expose you to new perspectives, challenge your assumptions, and provide encouragement during moments of self-doubt. Remember, developing a personal voice isn't about isolating yourself; it's about engaging with a community of like-minded individuals who share your passion for art.

Finally, remember that your artistic journey is a lifelong process. There will be moments of frustration, periods of self-doubt, and times when you feel lost or stuck. This is perfectly normal. Embrace these challenges as opportunities for growth. Don't be afraid to step outside your comfort zone, experiment with new approaches, and continually push the boundaries of your creative potential. The world of art is a vast and ever-evolving landscape, ripe with possibilities. Embrace the journey, trust your instincts, and let your unique voice shine through. Resources are abundant for artists seeking further inspiration and knowledge. Explore art books, online tutorials, museum collections, and artist interviews. Immerse yourself in the world of art, and allow it to fuel your creative fire.

7.1 Experimentation & Play

True mastery of any artistic skill transcends mere technical proficiency. It's about embracing the unexpected, allowing intuition to guide your hand, and finding joy in the process of discovery. This chapter, dedicated to experimentation and play, encourages you to push beyond the structured exercises and explore the boundless potential of line within your own unique artistic language. Think of your pen and brush not just as tools, but as extensions of your creative spirit, capable of whispering secrets onto the page. Let go of the need for perfection and embrace the happy accidents, the unexpected flourishes, the delightful imperfections that breathe life into your work.

One powerful approach to unlocking your creative potential is to limit your palette. Restricting yourself to a single pen or brush, a limited range of ink colors, or even just black and white can force you to focus on the nuances of line, texture, and composition. By removing the distraction of color choices, you can delve deeper into the expressive possibilities of line weight, direction, and rhythm. Try working with a single, fine-tipped pen on a large sheet of paper, exploring the subtle gradations of tone you can achieve through varying pressure and cross-hatching density. Or, experiment with a broad, flat brush and heavily diluted ink, allowing the watery washes to create unexpected textures and organic shapes. The limitations imposed by a restricted palette can paradoxically open up new avenues of creativity.

Another exciting avenue for experimentation lies in exploring unconventional drawing surfaces. Move beyond the smooth predictability of traditional drawing paper and embrace the textured world of found materials. Try sketching on rough watercolor paper, textured fabric, or even wood panels. The unique surface qualities of these materials will interact with your pen and brush in surprising ways, influencing the flow of ink and creating unexpected textures. Imagine the scratchy, broken lines achieved on coarse sandpaper, or the soft, diffuse marks created on absorbent canvas. These unconventional surfaces can add a unique dimension to your work, pushing you beyond your comfort zone and inspiring new artistic discoveries.

Embrace the power of unexpected combinations. Combine pen and brush in innovative ways, layering delicate ink washes beneath bold pen strokes or using the dry brush technique to create textured overlays on top of fluid ink lines. Experiment with incorporating other media into your linework, such as colored pencils, charcoal, or even collage elements. The interplay of different materials can create rich, complex surfaces and add depth to your artistic expression. Imagine the vibrant energy of a sketch where bold brushstrokes of color are interwoven with intricate pen details, or the subtle texture created by layering fragments of textured paper beneath delicate ink lines. Don't be afraid to break the rules and explore the unexpected harmonies that can arise from seemingly disparate elements.

Cultivate a spirit of playful exploration. Approach your drawing practice with a sense of childlike wonder, allowing yourself to experiment freely without judgment. Try blind contour drawing, where you draw the outline of a subject without looking at your paper, focusing solely on the tactile sensation of your pen or brush moving across the surface. Experiment with gesture drawing, capturing the essence of movement and energy in quick, fluid strokes. These exercises can help you loosen up, develop your hand-eye coordination, and cultivate a more intuitive approach to drawing. The freedom of play can unlock unexpected creative breakthroughs and lead you to discover new ways of seeing and expressing the world around you.

Engage with your surroundings. Draw inspiration from the natural world, from the intricate patterns of leaves and branches to the flowing forms of water and clouds. Observe the built environment, capturing the geometric precision of architecture or the dynamic energy of urban life. Even everyday objects can become fascinating subjects for exploration, revealing their hidden beauty through the careful observation and expressive rendering of line. By drawing from life, you not only sharpen your observational skills but also deepen your connection to the world around you. The act of translating three-dimensional reality into the two-dimensional language of line becomes a powerful form of visual storytelling.

Remember, the journey of artistic exploration is a deeply personal one. There is no right or wrong way to experiment and play. Embrace your individuality, allow your intuition to guide you, and trust the process of discovery. The more you experiment, the more you will develop your own unique artistic voice, a language of line that speaks directly from your heart and soul to the hearts and souls of others.

7.2 Developing a Personal Voice

Your artistic journey with pen and brush culminates in the discovery and cultivation of a personal voice. This is the stage where your technical proficiency transforms into genuine artistic expression. It's about infusing your work with your unique perspective, emotions, and experiences, moving beyond mere replication and into the realm of creation. Think of the masters – each identifiable not just by their subject matter but by the distinct way they wielded their tools. Their lines speak to us across centuries, whispering their individual stories. This chapter will guide you on this crucial path towards developing your own distinctive visual language.

One key aspect of developing your voice is consistent practice intertwined with mindful experimentation. Don't be afraid to push boundaries, try new approaches, and even make "mistakes." These so-called errors often lead to unexpected discoveries and can become integral parts of your style. Keep a sketchbook dedicated solely to experimentation. Fill it with textures, unusual line combinations, and unconventional mark-making. Treat it as a visual laboratory where you can freely explore the potential of your chosen media without the pressure of creating a finished piece. This consistent engagement, coupled with a willingness to venture outside your comfort zone, will gradually reveal your artistic inclinations.

Consider your subject matter. What draws your eye? What stories do you want to tell? Your personal voice isn't just about how you draw, but what you choose to draw. Are you captivated by the intricate details of nature? The bustling energy of urban scenes? The quiet introspection of portraits? Allow your passions to guide your artistic choices. Let your subject matter be a reflection of your inner world. This connection between your interests and your artwork will infuse your lines with authenticity and meaning, resonating with viewers on a deeper level.

Exploration of diverse artistic influences is crucial for growth and inspiration. Immerse yourself in the work of artists you admire. Study their techniques, but more importantly, analyze what resonates with you about their style. What qualities do you find compelling? How do they use line to convey emotion or narrative? Don't simply copy their work, but rather, internalize their approach and allow it to inform your own experimentation. Visit museums, explore online galleries, and delve into art books. Exposure to a wide range of artistic styles will broaden your visual vocabulary and help you identify elements that you can incorporate into your own unique language.

Your personal voice is also about recognizing and embracing your limitations. Every artist has strengths and weaknesses. Instead of viewing limitations as obstacles, consider them as opportunities to innovate. Perhaps you struggle with perfect precision. Embrace the looseness and expressiveness of gestural lines. Maybe you find intricate details overwhelming. Focus on capturing the essence of your subject through simplified forms and bold strokes. These "limitations" can become the defining characteristics of your style, setting your work apart and giving it a unique edge.

Don't underestimate the power of reflection and self-critique. Regularly assess your work. What are its strengths? Where can you improve? What feels authentic to you, and what seems forced or derivative? Honest self-assessment can be uncomfortable, but it's essential for growth. Seek feedback from trusted sources – fellow artists, mentors, or instructors. Be open to constructive criticism, but always filter it through your own artistic lens. Ultimately, the development of your personal voice is a deeply individual journey, and you are the ultimate judge of its authenticity.

The development of a personal voice is not a destination but an ongoing evolution. As you continue to practice, experiment, and refine your skills, your style will mature and deepen. Embrace the process. Allow your lines to become an extension of yourself, a visual manifestation of your unique perspective on the world. This continuous exploration and refinement is what makes the artistic journey so rewarding. It's in the ongoing pursuit of our unique voice that we truly discover the power and potential of our creative expression.

7.3 Resources & Inspiration

Fueling your creative journey requires more than just mastering techniques; it demands a constant influx of inspiration and a knowledge of the resources available to support your growth. Think of this chapter as your personalized toolkit, equipping you with the means to continually refine your linework and discover new avenues for artistic expression. We'll explore diverse sources of inspiration, from the natural world to the urban landscape, and delve into the wealth of resources available both online and in the real world. This is about expanding your horizons and cultivating a lifelong passion for the art of line.

Begin with the world around you. Observe the intricate patterns in nature – the veining of a leaf, the ripples in water, the texture of bark. These organic forms offer an endless wellspring of inspiration for your linework. Consider sketching these patterns directly, focusing on capturing their essence with varying line weights and rhythms. Urban environments provide a contrasting yet equally rich source of inspiration. The geometric lines of buildings, the chaotic tangle of wires, the rhythmic flow of traffic – all offer unique opportunities to explore line in dynamic and unexpected ways. Sketching on location, even for short periods, can dramatically enhance your ability to see and interpret line in the world around you.

Expand your visual library by actively seeking out the work of established artists. Explore different artistic movements and styles, paying close attention to how artists have utilized line to create mood, texture, and depth. Don't limit yourself to pen and brush artists; look at the linework in etchings, engravings, woodcuts, and even calligraphy. Each medium offers unique insights into the expressive potential of line. Visit museums, galleries, and libraries to experience artwork firsthand. The tactile experience of seeing original artwork can be profoundly inspiring, offering a deeper understanding of an artist's technique and vision.

Immerse yourself in the vast resources available online. Art blogs, online communities, and social media platforms dedicated to drawing and illustration offer a constant stream of inspiration and opportunities to connect with fellow artists. Online tutorials and workshops can provide valuable instruction in specific techniques, while digital libraries and archives offer access to a wealth of historical and contemporary artwork. Be discerning in your online explorations, focusing on resources that resonate with your artistic interests and goals.

Explore the world of print. Books on drawing, illustration, and art history provide a more in-depth exploration of techniques, concepts, and artistic movements. Seek out books that focus specifically on linework, exploring its use in different contexts and styles. Art magazines and journals offer contemporary perspectives on the art world, showcasing the work of emerging and established artists. Building a personal library of inspiring resources can provide a constant source of motivation and guidance throughout your artistic journey.

Experiment with different drawing tools and materials. Explore various pen nibs, brush types, inks, and papers to discover the unique qualities each offers. The tactile experience of working with different materials can spark new ideas and inspire different approaches to your linework. Don't be afraid to step outside your comfort zone and try something new. Unexpected discoveries often arise from experimentation.

Connect with other artists. Joining a local art group, attending workshops, or participating in online communities can provide valuable opportunities for feedback, encouragement, and inspiration. Sharing your work and engaging in discussions with other artists can broaden your perspective and help you refine your artistic vision. The exchange of ideas and perspectives can be a powerful catalyst for growth.

Consider attending workshops or taking classes. Learning from experienced instructors can provide valuable insights into specific techniques and approaches to linework. The structured environment of a workshop or class can help you focus your efforts and accelerate your learning. Even short-term workshops can provide a significant boost to your skills and inspiration.

Maintain a sketchbook as a visual diary of your artistic journey. Use it to capture fleeting moments of inspiration, experiment with new techniques, and develop your ideas. Your sketchbook can serve as a valuable record of your progress and a source of inspiration for future projects. Don't be afraid to fill your sketchbook with quick sketches, doodles, and notes. These seemingly insignificant markings can often lead to unexpected breakthroughs.

Cultivate a mindset of continuous learning and exploration. The journey of artistic development is an ongoing process of discovery. Embrace challenges, experiment with new ideas, and never stop seeking inspiration. The more you invest in your artistic growth, the more rewarding your creative journey will become. Remember, the power of line lies in its ability to communicate emotion, tell stories, and capture the essence of the world around us. By continually refining your understanding of line and exploring its expressive potential, you can unlock new levels of creativity and develop a unique artistic voice.

www.ingramcontent.com/pod-product-compliance
Ingram Content Group UK Ltd.
Pitfield, Milton Keynes, MK11 3LW, UK
UKHW031023120325
4954UKWH00010B/411

* 9 7 9 8 3 4 8 4 6 2 5 1 2 *